TABLE OF CONTENTS

INTRODUCTION

Dark psychology generally refers to the use of mind control tactics to influence a people's thinking and behavior, and in so doing make them do what the manipulator want. A manipulator will identify weak links in their target's reasoning and use it gaps to sneak into their mind to prey on them. Manipulators understand that there is bound to be some resistance from their target, and for this reason, they have since developed new and unique tactics to further their course. It is for this reason that we must equip you with the latest techniques being used in the secret world of dark psychology to control minds.

Knowing the fundamentals of dark psychology is not necessarily meant to turn you to a psychopath, narcissist or sociopath, but these little tricks will come in handy whenever you're confronted by situations that demand their use. The main purpose of bringing these techniques to your doorstep, however, is to serve as a deterrent against mind manipulation. Those who know very little or nothing about the techniques used in dark psychology stand the risk of it being used against them big time. Psychopaths and narcissists are not happy with you learning these tricks because they won't be having an advantage over you any longer.

The irony with dark psychology is that the manipulator uses you as a weapon against yourself; all for their benefit! It is important that you get informed that manipulators can do little or nothing at all to you if they can't access your mind. If you make the mistake of letting them hijack your mind, you become a mere robot that does anything and everything they want. The world today is full of such robots and their masters are the people with the knowledge of dark psychology. These people are incorrectly presumed to possess magical powers.

By the time you are done reading this book, you will realize that there is nothing magical about their 'power'. In any case, you will acquire abilities just like theirs and you will in a better position to understand how and why they do it.

CHAPTER 1: THE BASICS OF DARK PSYCHOLOGY

The basics of dark psychology are the fundamental principles and techniques used by manipulators in their step-by-step process to manipulate, influence, and control people's minds. We shall look at these principles from the victim's point of view to make them even easier for you to understand.

Motivating Action and Illusion of Free Will

Motivating action is the attempt by a manipulator to impose their ideas on the target and make it look like it is the victim's idea. After carefully identifying their target, the manipulator starts laying the ground for manipulation before they make contact. Once contact has been established, all their actions, including every single word they speak, bring them closer to their goal of manipulating the target.

Every manipulator understands that human beings are naturally inclined to give contradictory statements and opinions even when they know those arguments wrong or misplaced. A manipulator will use this rationale weakness in human reasoning to their full advantage. They will lay traps which you will fall into unsuspectingly.

Manipulators have mastered the art of turning their ideas into 'yours'. One outstanding feature of the relationship between you and the manipulator during the first encounter is contrasting ideas and opinions. They will find a way sneaking into your mind using various techniques that include asking mind-provoking question and intimidation. Before you know it both of you will be having the same ideas and opinions, which on close scrutiny turn out to be theirs. It takes them less than three meetings to know how your mind works and thus decide the most appropriate methods to use on you, starting from basic ones. If you prove to be a hard nut to crack, the manipulator will employ more complex and dangerous techniques until they succeed in manipulating you. The following are the basic techniques employed in the secret world of dark psychology to manipulate people.

Concealment

Just like a cheetah's concealed stalk through the grassland, waiting for the right time to pounce on its prey, a manipulator will conceal their motive from the beginning. You will notice elements of concealment from the following ways:

    a. **They won't ask direct questions**. Their famous strategy is floating an idea to you and when you give a response, they twist will and modify it to align with their line of thought.

    b. **They will avoid certain questions in a clever way**. A manipulator will either pretend not to have heard a question or answer it anyway but in an irrelevant way. In some cases, the answers they give are way too vague to offer any help.

    c. **Your interests are their 'top priority'**. No one sounds as selfless as a person that wants to manipulate you. Whenever you interact with them, they create an illusion that it is all about you; your interests, your needs and your beliefs. They will 'protect' all your interests like a guardian angel. This way, they know they can easily gain your trust and be in a better position to manipulate you.

d. **Being selfish with information.** Before a manipulator approaches you, they make sure they have fore-knowledge of the amount of information at your disposal. If you are not well-informed about a specific matter, they will praise your little grasp of the topic to give you false confidence while hiding the most vital information from you at the same time.

e. **Acting dumb**. Manipulators are some of the best actors the world has ever seen. By the time you are done dealing with one, or let us say by the time he is done dealing with you, you will be left with the memory of a shadow. They will fake everything from their personality to their level of thinking. You might think you are helping them understand something while you are actually walking right into a trap.

Impairment of critical thinking capacity

A manipulator will try to take away your ability to obey your conscience and guard your interests. Manipulators will hack the process of critical thinking and deny you the freedom of making independent decisions. The predator makes your brain bypass its normal inspection process before decision-making; they achieve this fete of destabilizing your mind by using distorted facts alongside their notoriously skewed reasoning. They present manipulated arguments about the subject of contention because they know you will unlikely give an objection due to your impaired thinking. To compound the basics of dark psychology, we are going to use a very short example for illustration.

Disclaimer: All examples and illustrations we shall be using are not meant to undermine any religion or ideology, neither are they a reflection of the writer's opinions and beliefs. They are entirely for educational purposes.

A cultist would approach you with the intention of making you join their cult. From the word go, they know that you won't accept the offer if they approached you directly, but since they are very cunning, they would likely tackle you in this manner:

CULTIST: Do you know that there is a God?

YOU: Yes. I know… he is somewhere up there.

CULTIST: I can't wait to go to heaven. Nobody else has done that in our time.

YOU: The dead are in heaven already, the souls of the righteous.

CULTIST: That is correct, but not the real heaven, they're somewhere in between.

YOU: How do you know that?

CULTIST: I have a friend, who died for some minutes, he came back after we prayed for him.

YOU: Impossible!

CULTIST: What do you mean impossible? I thought you are a believer, don't you believe in prayers?

YOU: I do, but…

CULTIST: He has been giving testimonies in our prayer meetings.

YOU: Oh yeah?

CULTIST: My cousin has been nagging me to take her to hear it for herself. I took her there last week.

YOU: I'm curious.

CULTIST: I can take you too, this Friday.

YOU: Maybe, I'll think about it.

The conversation above looks very normal from face value.

However, there is so much manipulation hidden between the lines.

It will take a sharp mind and knowledge of dark psychology to identify elements of manipulation. The cultist has achieved several objectives in less than a minute by impairing your ability to think critically.

He has made you believe there is a god without giving you a chance to clarify the kind of God you two are referring to. The aspect of religion is common to both of you but the finer details are not addressed.

The cultist has perfectly concealed his motive. Normally, a religious person is presumed to be morally upright. If someone starts a conversation and 'God' is in the first sentence, it boosts the level of trust and respect they will be accorded. This is exactly what the cultist has done.

There is a lot of vagueness in the cultist's reasoning. He says that dead people go somewhere in between. This statement is misleading from the beginning, but since he started it with matters to do with faith, he had a free pass. If you had a chance to think critically, you would know that most established religions have a heaven and hell, nothing in between. The mere mention of something between should have been a red flag. But again, he made you believe that it is not entirely their idea nor did he confirm that the source was initially a member of their 'group' before he died.

He makes you think that since you are entitled to know more information about your faith, you wouldn't mind accompanying him on Friday to his 'prayer group'. This looks like your initiative when it is indeed theirs.

At the end of the day, you will join their prayer group to 'hear for yourself'. Before you get there, they will be waiting for you and they know exactly what you will be looking for. They will avail it and you will consume it to your satisfaction. Everything you will be asked to do from that point will be a laid trap. You will be in with both legs before you know it; the power of dark psychology.

These points will summarize the basic features of dark psychology. Keep them at the back of your mind as we shall be revisiting and expounding them in the course of this book.

1. Mind controlling is a motivating action.

2. A tendency to create an illusion that everything, especially the matter of contention, is the idea of the target. This leaves little or no room for objection and resistance.

3. A psychopath or narcissist employs morally questionable tactics that are marred by misdirection, misinformation, and threats.

4. There is a deliberate interruption of critical thinking by the manipulator in ways that don't raise suspicion.

5. The manipulator guards all the interests of the target for as long as their objective is not met.

6. A weak link is created between rational reasoning and objective reasoning to weaken the target's inspection ability.

INTERMEDIATE TECHNIQUES

Like I said before, these techniques are not entirely meant for psychopaths and narcissists. They will come in handy at one point in your life, be it in a preventive or any other way. Intermediate techniques are those methods used by manipulators immediately after sneaking into your personal space and gaining your trust. Some of these techniques are discussed below. The techniques are applied to different personalities after assessment by the predator; they are not necessarily uniform to everyone. The techniques are also always undergoing modification by dark psychologists to suit different situations. Politicians, for instance, use prevailing economic and political situations to come up with new tricks to lure voters. Black magicians and cultists, on the other hand, use the most current tragedies to instill fear in their subjects. The techniques are also unique to different communities and cultures.

Dark psychologists are experts in applying tactics that suit their situation.

Lies

Psychopaths will always mislead their target in virtually every way. These lies start right from things about their personal lives to their beliefs and convictions. Once they lie to you, you will get confused and end up taking a different route of reasoning. They then use this gap in your reasoning to manipulate you in a way that serves their interests. When a lie is told over and over again, it gradually transforms into a half-truth before finally appearing like a 'truth' to the victim. To get the lie this far, a dark psychologist will ensure consistency in their lying.

Vagueness

A manipulator will not give you the whole story. They make sure that every piece of information they give is lacking the fundamental gist. You won't be able to extract any sensibility from the story. This creates a perfect environment for them to feed you manipulative ideas, ideas that comprise many half-truths or no truth at all. Their stories and ideas are also incoherent. It will take you a lot of time trying to reconstruct the many pieces of information to come up with a story that makes sense. This becomes a delaying tactic as well as a distraction from the main objective by the manipulator.

Feigning Love

Psychopaths and narcissists will go on a charm offensive to lure their victims into thinking that they have their best interests at heart. Anybody would naturally relax in such a relationship and their reasoning is reduced. A level of trust is also built. This reduces objection and resistance by the victim. If someone starts warming towards you for no apparent reason, just know that they are after something. It is a ticking time-bomb that will destroy you. Look out for suspicious affection by someone you barely know or by someone that has not been all that nice before. Normally, they will use and dump you in the most inhumane way immediately their objective is met. It will go as fast as it came.

Unpredictable Moods

Manipulators normally have varying moods as dictated by their predetermined goals. Sometimes these mood swings are so weird that they not change within short intervals but also have extremities. One minute they are very happy and the next one they will be bursting with anger. Surprisingly, these mood swings are deliberate; it is nothing close to their personality. This is a technique they use to put you off balance. Once they get you started on the wrong foot, it will be difficult for you to detect their next move. Usually, you will find them in their real mood but it suddenly changes to suit the situation, the ideal situation they plan to manipulate you in.

Denial

A manipulator will deny anything that raises eyebrows about their intention. They will assure you that such a thing will never happen. The denial comes every time you talk about the possibility of a negative outcome. If they plan to include you in a dubious business deal, for instance, they will keep refusing the fact that anything might go wrong. They will tell you that nothing wrong will happen whatsoever even when you know it is obvious things don't always go as planned.

Threats

A psychopath sometimes goes to the extent of forcing you to do what they want in an indirect way and warning of the consequences of not doing it. Their tone is characterized by a lot of nagging, shouting and begging. If the situation is dire, they might even resort to physical violence or threaten to use violence. This is normally a desperate measure they apply when they sense that their plan might hit a dead end. Once their target feels threatened, they start doing things out of fear rather than being driven by conscience. This allows the manipulator to exploit that missing link in reasoning to their advantage.

False Accusations

A predator will insinuate that everything that goes wrong is your fault. They will also find fault in virtually everything you do. This is a strategy meant to tear you apart. You will likely end up losing your self-esteem and have feelings of guilt. Again, they have thrown you off balance. They will then create an illusion of perfection on their part. This way, everything they suggest will have a free pass since they have killed the possibility of objection.

Spinning the Truth

Manipulators are experts when it comes to spinning the truth. They will manipulate and twist facts for their benefit. At face value, what they tell you to look like the truth but when you read between the lines, you will notice missing links. They deliberately do this to minimize your level of a grasp on the issue at hand. They also do this as a way of disguising bad behavior. Having succeeded in keeping you in the dark, your mind will be theirs to manipulate at will. Even when you manage to uncover the truth by yourself, they will still have a way of poking holes in it to align it with their version.

Minimizing

Manipulators will deliberately put themselves at a disadvantage when it comes to the level of the grasp of the information. They do this by making errors in their reasoning, just to provoke a reaction from you. If you give a correct line of reasoning about the subject matter, they will taint it with their crooked thinking and that is when your good thinking starts degenerating to their 'level'. They will then manipulate you without a trickle of sweat since you are not the thinker you were a while ago.

Isolation

Psychopaths, narcissists, and sociopaths will isolate the victim from every other source of influence but them. They will cut you off from your friends, peers, and family. Isolating you gives them a chance to control all information and ideas coming into your mind. This way, they will be able to feed you their ideas from left, right and center. The isolation comes in the form of seminars and workshops where a group of people would be kept indoors for periods those even last months. They are brainwashed and reeducated until they abandon their initial positions. By the time they are released, they will be completely hooked to the manipulator's line of thinking and reasoning. This method has been especially employed by pyramid schemes to nab their victims and turn them into zombies. These are the majority of people that work at the bottom off the pyramid to benefit the minority at the top.

Aggression

Dark psychologists have an over-the-top aggressive habit that is meant to defocus the target. The aggression which comes in the form of anger, threats, and deep withdrawal is meant to reduce resistance and objection. This deliberately manufactured problem makes the victim look for a solution to it first. This distracts them from the real intentions of the prey. If the manipulator acts angry, for instance, the target will first calm them down before paying attention to anything else. In the end, the predator gets a free pass just by distracting the target with the 'anger'.

Innocence

Manipulators are also experts in playing the innocent. This strategy is meant to soften the ground as the target will tread carefully when handling them. Innocence is also a tool they use to reduce resistance. The target will question their judgment every time the predator reacts to a response with innocence. Before you know it, you will be thinking just as they expect and doing what they ask of you.

Sarcastic Comments

Manipulators use this strategy to strip their target of self-dignity and lower their self-esteem. This normally happens when the victim is in the company of others as this is the best time to prick their confidence. Once this is done, the target is robbed of freedom of thinking independently and freely. Hurting their ego will also create fear for the manipulator. The victim will do anything they are told and agree to ideas to avoid worsening the situation.

Flattery

Human beings naturally like being praised. It gives them a sense of self-worth and increases their self-confidence immensely. A dark psychologist is aware of this weakness and will exploit it to the maximum. They will shower the victim with praises and even give credit where it is due. This strategy is magical in earning their trust. Once the manipulator is trusted, most off their suggestions will go unchallenged because the target expects more praise from them.

Avoidance

Dark psychologists will do everything in their power to mislead the target and conceal their true intentions. This is achieved through diversion and avoidance of sensitive topics. As soon as the matter of contention is touched, the manipulator will hastily create a new topic as a diversionary measure. This will happen as its objective is not met. They also avoid tackling matters directly such as giving direct answers to direct questions. Virtually all their responses are irrelevant and vague. It is easy to tell when they are up to something from their avoidance of topics.

Feigning Empathy

Naturally, dark psychologists are among the most heartless and insensitive to the human race. However, they will fake their feelings for you just to earn your trust. They will provoke you into the opening of your problems. They will then pretend to feel bad about your issues while in actual sense they are digging to know your weaknesses. They will then use them against you without your knowledge. You will think they are kind and caring but when they get what they want, they drop you like a hot iron bar.

Guilt Tripping

A manipulator will set numerous traps for their victim to make them feel guilty even when they are the ones at fault. This serves to make the victim more confused and anxious. They will be careful not to do anything that might hurt the feelings of the manipulator. This kind of sensitivity on the part of the victim dispels feelings of selfishness and makes them put aside their interests first. Again, the manipulator wins by using the victim against themselves.

Suspicious Generosity

A manipulator will go to greater lengths while trying to please the victim. This strategy involves the flow of expensive gifts like presents, meals, gadgets and sometimes money. This is meant to buy the victim's friendship especially in cases where such friendship would not blossom naturally. Once they win the victim's heart, it is where they will proceed to the mind. It is easy to tell when such kind of generosity is suspicious. The gifts and favors will start reducing as time goes by. Every favor brings them a step to their objective. This comes to an abrupt ending when their objective is finally met.

Endless Games

A manipulator will play the victim's mind in the most gruesome way. This kind of game is characterized by endless lies and promises that never get fulfilled. This technique is meant to buy more time for the predator. It is also a tool used to create a false profile of the manipulator. The lies are designed to align with the expectations of the target and thus give them some false satisfaction. These games will under modifications from time to time to suit new circumstances and situations. A unique characteristic of these games is that they are so accurate and consistent that it becomes difficult to detect them.

Targeting the Victim

Attacks directed at the victim are meant to put them on the defensive. This serves the purpose of diverting their attention from the manipulation. The victim spends more time explaining themselves instead of looking out for the motive behind the attacks. Such attacks and accusations become severe as time goes by until the objective of the predator is met. It is not hard to detect baseless accusations directed to you by the would-be manipulator. Most of the attacks are emotionally driven and in bad faith. If it is happening at work by a boss that does not want you anymore, you will notice that the accusations or attacks are not correctional. They are more provocative and demeaning in a way that will make you look arrogant and disrespectful. The boss will then use this latter reason to fire you, and this gives them an even strong case against you. Technically, they have used you to fire yourself through mind manipulation.

These intermediate techniques do not give dark psychologists enough power to manipulate you. That's why you need to get to know the advanced techniques they use in the next chapter.

ADVANCED TECHNIQUES

Dark psychologists apply intense and more powerful techniques on their victims when the previous methods fail to work. These advanced tactics are designed to give the target one last blow after several failed attempts. They are more technical and ruthless compared to the previous basic and intermediate techniques. You must get familiar with all these methods, it is only then that you will be or close to be on the same footing as the dark psychologists. These advanced tactics used by psychopaths, sociopaths, and narcissists are discussed below.

Brainwashing

This is a broad and very complicated strategy used by manipulators to bring you to your knees before using you to advance their agenda. The tactic involves complete and total reeducation of the target to shift their moral standing. Technically, it is hijacking the whole personality of the victim without their knowledge. In so doing, a completely different identity is planted on the person to suit the manipulator's interests. Brainwashing has the following characteristics:

Breaks down the old you- this involves the

manipulator doing away with your old self. This is done by making you disregard your beliefs and convictions completely. They would find fault in the things you used to believe in and in the way you did things. The loss of principles leaves you exposed and vulnerable. Remember a person's principles are like a compass that shows the direction in terms of reasoning and behavior. If this fundamental ability to stand your ground is taken away from you, a vacuum is created that needs to be filled. You can guess what the manipulator would use to fill that gap.

Crushes the victim's identity- dark psychologists

will then make a move at your identity. They will be pricking your ego by systematically attacking your personality in a very provocative manner until you become disoriented. Prisoners of war have fallen prey to these kinds of attacks where their captors tell them everything they are not and everything they are fighting for. They are labeled slaves of their ideologies. Some of them are even told to their faces that they are not real men or women. This makes you feel worthless and unworthy. A degenerated self-esteem strips you of your dignity and leaves you at their mercy.

Imposes feelings of guilt- a wounded personality or identity becomes more susceptible to feelings of guilt. The victim now starts hating who they are and become overly ashamed of themselves. Manipulators have perfected the art of fueling these feelings of guilt. They will make their victims believe that it is their fault that they are inferior. They will stress that indeed the victim had a choice about what was good for them but they ended up choosing the wrong things. And since the victim had already been stripped of the ability to defend their identity, they will take the manipulator's word for it. Both of them now team up to attack and blame the victim's old self.

Betrayal- after feeling guilty of their identity, the victim now starts disowning their previous identity. They will find fault in their previous choices even when they could see no fault at all. Everything they have ever done becomes useless and misleading. The victim drowns in their guilt and confesses that they are bad.

Identity crisis- the victim has reached a breaking point. They become completely disoriented and confused. They completely forget who they are and what their purpose is as feelings of shame run through them. At this point, the person would fall for anything that would offer them the slightest consolation. They have lost trust in themselves and are afraid of making any more decisions by themselves. The victim loses grip of reality, they might also sink in depression. Some of them would get overwhelmed and start crying.

A ray of hope- as their target undergoes all the emotional anguish as a result of losing their identity, the predator will be waiting for them to drop dead as a vulture does. They decide to

intervene once they realize that their victim has hit rock bottom.
They will float the idea of the possibility of salvation once the
victim reaches that breaking point. By now they are certain that the
victim will not turn down their offer. They see it as the only
opportunity to save them from sinking to identity oblivion.
However, the promise of salvation comes with a long list of
conditions to the victim. One outstanding condition will be for the
victim to turn away from their former ways. This includes
abandoning their previous beliefs and principles. The manipulator
presents their ideas as the only way out for the victim. The victim
is not given much choice and they have no say regarding their new
identity. Everything about the new identity will be as designed by
the manipulator.

As the brainwashing process nears completion, the target
undergoes these stages:

· Leniency is the first stage of salvation. The manipulator starts by
offering to remove the victim from that situation of hopelessness,
shame, and guilt. If the victim feels some relief from the possibility
of being saved, the manipulator then proceeds to state their

demands as a favor they need from the victim in return. This stage is also characterized by material gifts and offers such as food, drinks, and money aimed at making the victim feel better. The material offers are also meant to boost the level of trust the victim has on the manipulator.

· The second stage is the compulsion to confession. Here, the manipulator makes their subject see the possibility of helping themselves with only a little help from them. The dark psychologist motivates the victim to assert their desire to come out of their situation and build a new self. Having been presented with the choice of helping themselves, the victim feels obliged to right their past wrongs. They also feel the need to not disappoint their 'Savior' who have volunteered to 'help' them out.

· Channeling of guilt becomes the third stage. Here, the manipulator attaches the guilt the victim has been feeling to their old self. The victim is not able to explain the origin of the feelings of guilt at this point. And this is where the manipulator comes with their dubious explanations. In the course of these explanations, a contrast is created between the old set of beliefs and the new ones.

The victim's old beliefs will be used as the scapegoat for all the suffering the victim has been undergoing. The new set, on the other hand, will be portrayed as a ticket to a better future full of glory.

· The fourth step involves releasing guilt. The victim is now convinced that their old set of beliefs is the cause of suffering and that they are ready to let go of them. At this stage, the desire for a new identity is unstoppable. The victim has no second thoughts about the change they are about to execute. The level of brainwashing has become so severe that they don't stop to think if there is something good in the old self that needs to be carried along to the new identity. They also don't analyze the new offer critically to see if there are any shortcomings associated with it. All they want to do is bury the old self and become something else, completely new.

· The person starts rebuilding themselves. After doing away with the old identity, the victim embarks on rebuilding and restructuring themselves according to the manipulator's manual. The instructions in that manual are supposed to suit the predator's interests 100 percent. The victim has no share in the new person they are building. They are just serving robots with the manipulator as their master. The victim feels that they owe the manipulator for fixing their brokenness. This is enough reason to do anything they are asked without objection. The manipulator sees this as a perfect opportunity to implant their version of ideas in the victim with certainty that there won't be any objection.

· The last stage of brainwashing is harmony with the new self and starting over. The new identity comes with calm and comfort for the victim after a period of emotional disturbance. The dark psychologist makes this appear like the victim's choice and initiative to build a new self. Technically, the choice was made for them when the old ways were demonized and the new ones praised by the manipulator. The victim would naturally choose the latter but the choice was clinically imposed on them. After finding comfort in the thought of following this new path, the victim embarks on a journey to put the new beliefs into practice. The manipulator becomes their new 'mentor' as they start the journey.

Metacommunication

This is a strategy used in the world of dark psychology where the manipulator uses a stream of subliminal messages on their target. These messages are implanted in the subject's mind during long indoctrination lectures. The messages in the form of short statements and slogans are repeated over and over until they stick in the victim's mind. The human mind is programmed to recall and familiarize more with repeated things. In such lectures, most of the contents are unrelated to the manipulator's aim but they serve as a way of relaying a message contained in the subliminal remarks. The message can be coded or just bare depending on its sensitivity. For example, a black magician would use words like 'for nothing happens without blood sacrifice' severally in the middle of their chanting to insinuate that the target needs to familiarize themselves with the issue of blood sacrifice. If these words are repeated over and over again, your mind will stick to them despite having heard many more words in the chant. This is meant to wire your brain into giving more thought to the words. Once you start entertaining the thought, your curiosity will be awakened. You might start considering the words every time you are faced with a dire problem that needs to be solved immediately.

Politicians have also created slogans to advance their agenda. The world of dark psychology uses such slogans to manipulate and influence masses to their advantage. The Nazis, for example, created slogans that fueled their anti-Semitic agenda before and during the Second World War. Every time such slogans were used in public meetings and rallies, feelings of hatred would run high among the crowds. People would then leave the meetings with charged emotions and end up harming those people whom the slogans targeted. This is the reason some of those slogans and accompanying gestures such as "hail Hitler" came to be banned by governments of the world after the war was over. They caused more psychological harm to the victims in greater numbers than the ones harmed physically.

Disinhibition

This tactic is used by dark psychologists to control the minds of their subjects by making them look inferior. It is a technique that is mostly used by a cultist. The subject is encouraged to obey and follow like a child. The manipulator elevates them to a more superior position to instill fear rather than command respect. The victim is presented with two options when it comes to obedience; obey and benefit from it or refuse and suffer the consequences. To give more weight to this rule, the manipulator devices ways of punishing those who don't obey them and even goes to the extent of punishing them to drive the point home.

In some religious settings, coinciding tragic events are used to instill fear on the masses and force them to do certain things. This normally happens when they want to extort the subject. They will wait for a misfortune to befall you and then use it to advance their agenda. They would tell you things like, 'your child got sick because you have refused to give a certain amount of money'. This statement is accompanied by a 'solution' that also serves as a warning; 'if you give the money, the child will get well, if you don't, and more misfortunes will come your way'. This obedience of a child allows the manipulator to make demands on you at will for as long as they want.

Rigid rules

A manipulator will set extremely strict conditions and rules that can only be compared to a dictatorship. These rules are designed to guide the target to each of the laid traps. Bending these rules has the potential of jeopardizing the whole process so they will avoid it at all costs. The unbending rules are also meant to create limited time for thinking and action by the target. They are left with the easier option of following the rules as they are. Every time the victim tries to negotiate about changing or modifying the rules, they either get ignored or threatened altogether. Sometimes the bureaucracy attached to changing the rules is too hectic and weary that the target would normally give up before making any significant gains. Corrupt government officials, for instance, would come up with a complex channel of communication or network of financial flow that would make it difficult to trace looted funds. Since the human mind is susceptible to fatigued, the victim gives up after just a few attempts. Rigid rules should always be a red flag whenever you come across them. They are likely masking a form of manipulation.

Sleep deprivation

It is funny how people respond to things in their sleep irrespective. I once asked a friend that was half-asleep if I could borrow their phone. The sleep was becoming so heavy that he just murmured a 'yes' to my request. Two hours later he woke up and found me using the phone. He asked, 'who gave you permission to use my phone?' I answered, 'you did'. He insisted that he didn't give out permission. I smiled and gave the phone back. There is a tendency for the brain to refuse to work properly when someone is asleep or wants to sleep. The brain's activity slows down when someone wants to sleep. It is even worse if you have not had enough sleep for a long time. The level of the brain's refusal to think can be compared to a total shutdown. A manipulator understands this phenomenon very well and will exploit it to the maximum. They will approach you when your brain is less active due to prolonged lack of sleep. They will then manipulate your thoughts and implant their ideas on you without much resistance. They might even go the extra mile of engaging you in some mental or physical activity that will make your brain even more tired. The mind is more vulnerable at this point.

Blackmail

This is an act of coercion that involves the use of threats to achieve a certain objective. A manipulator will target the victim's property, money and threaten to harm them or people that are close to them. This can also be viewed as a form of extortion. Dark psychologists will use this strategy to force their way into the mind of the target. Before resorting to blackmail, it means the manipulator has exhausted almost every other method but seems to have hit a dead end, so this becomes a desperate move at the target. When at times the target doesn't give in to the demand, this desperation pushes the psychopath to make real their threats. In a way, this is a win situation for the target even though they might have incurred losses of property or having their loved ones harmed. Terrorists and criminals have been known to employ this technique to manipulate their victims. Smart governments that have noticed this kind of manipulation have come up with policies of zero tolerance to such manipulation. The United States government, for example, has a slogan, 'we do not negotiate with terrorists' even when those terrorists are holding hostages. This method has proven to be effective in the fight against terrorism since not giving in to their demands defeats their ideology. Imagine how many attacks and hostage-taking situations would be occurring if their wishes were granted every time they do that. My advice to you if someone tries to blackmail you is that you'd rather lose that property than lose your freedom of mind forever.

Familiarizing yourself with these advanced techniques used in the world of dark psychology will equip you with the knowledge and skills to guard yourself against mind control and manipulation. Like I said before, these skills are not meant to train you to be a psychopath but they will come in handy when the situation demands.

READING PEOPLE'S MINDS FROM THEIR WORDS

Words are an expression of an individual's thoughts and emotions. No matter how much someone tries to hide what is in their mind, their words will always betray them in one way or another. The world of dark psychology employs this technique to get into people's minds and perform wonders on them. When it comes to the meaning of words, dark psychology does not pay attention to the literal meaning of those words; it is never related to meanings found in the dictionary. What someone will look for is the actual meaning coming from within the speaker; what is really in their mind. The following combination of factors will help you decipher the actual meaning in the words of the target.

Pitch

This is the pitch in the speaker's speech. Do they say some words with a high voice and others with a low one? The tone with which words are said speaks volumes about the feelings and thoughts of an individual. Let us look at the following example; a politician and presenter are having a chat on national television.

POLITICIAN: the citizens must be excited that I'm selling my manifestos here today.

PRESENTER: oh yeah? It is expected.

POLITICIAN: My social media pages are flooding with messages of goodwill (low); my opponents must see that (high).

PRESENTER: but first let us hear what you have in store for the people.

POLITICIAN: most of them already know my agendas, but I will state them again, anyway.

PRESENTER: You can't be so sure, sir. It is your first time on-air; this is a good opportunity to boost your popularity (low).

POLITICIAN: (whispering) very well, I didn't know I'm not known.

PRESENTER: hey, just not enough (low).

(The politician sighs)

From this dialogue, we see that the politician is trying hard to make the presenter believe that he is popular while he is not. He cunningly tries to avoid addressing the issues directly by using general words like 'agendas' and 'manifestos'. He manipulates his way into the presenter's mind and finds the truth-he is not all that popular. The use of the words 'citizens' 'the people' and 'social media' indicate that the politician is targeting popularity. We can also get to read the politician's mind from the pitch in his voice. He says his social media pages are flooding with messages of goodwill with a low voice, an indication that he desperately needs the fame he is talking about. The low voice means the 'flooding' is a mere exaggeration. The second part of that statement is more of a threat directed at his opponents, some sort of propaganda, 'my opponents must see'. The use of the word 'must' about his opponents tells us that he is just bluffing. He has no control over what his opponents should or should not do whatsoever.

Pick Cues

Sometimes the speaker does not bring out their thoughts using the right words. They will use a variety of synonyms and other techniques to deliberately mislead the listener. Dark psychologists will pick these cues from the words spoken and use them to accurately read the speaker's mind. Let us look at the following examples.

"After the wedding, I patiently waited in the queue until I got served."

The clue here is the word 'patiently'. This statement means the speaker was not only hungry but they also had no alternative other than following the long queue to the end. It says a lot about their financial position as well as the significance of that event to them. This information can be used to press the right buttons if the person is to be manipulated into doing something they'd otherwise not agree to easily. You could promise such a person plenty of food or financial assistance as a way of winning them. Here is another practical example:

"Not that I'm afraid of heights, I just don't trust our engineers."

These are the words of someone that is afraid of heights but finds a good excuse to cover it up. The mention of the word 'afraid' is enough evidence of the underlying fear. This fact is reinforced by the kind of reason they give. Technically, all buildings have not been built by one person and unless it is condemned, then there is no cause for alarm. And does it mean the person will never enter a high-story building? Not, the bottom line here is the person is afraid of heights. You can easily use this weakness on their part to manipulate them.

The trick when it comes to picking cues is no analyzing every word spoken by someone in a sentence. Relate every word with the previous and subsequent one to get its meaning and context. This will help you to identify misplaced words that will serve as cues. The cues will, in turn, put you in a better position to read someone's mind quite easily.

Look out for repetitions

Words that are repeated over and over again are something to pay attention to if you are looking to discover what is in someone's mind. It means the speaker is desperately trying to communicate their thoughts but they do so in a way that people will not understand. These words can be synonyms or related sentiments so it takes a lot of careful evaluation to identify. Look at the following three statements.

I would love to have a big car when I find a good job.

My mum would have bought an expensive dress if my neighbor's daughter's graduation was mine.

I watched an action movie with robots that built castles in the sky. The three sentences have a consistent similarity in that they are centered on big things, luxurious ones for that matter. These things are the person's biggest fantasies. If you analyze the sentences keenly, you will notice that the words 'big', 'expensive', and 'sky' are related. They all have something to do with success. This tells us that the speaker has a strong desire to live largely. It also tells us that their current condition is nowhere near their fantasies. This intense craving for material success can be used to manipulate such an individual. Dark psychologists would listen to someone speak, not to understand them but to notice those words that person keeps emphasizing.

THE LINK BETWEEN SPEECH AND BODY LANGUAGE

To effectively hack someone's mind, you must learn to pay attention to every single detail concerning the word they utter and accompanying body movements. The words they use are major cues people use to express their thoughts. Body movements are just mere reinforcements for those words. Try to create a connection between every word spoken and the accompanying movement, these two could occur simultaneously or separately. Learning to relate words and movements will come in handy when looking out for people that want to manipulate you. We shall study single words and movements in this chapter as a technique of paying attention to details. This will be illustrative for ease of understanding.

Words and Accompanying Body Movements

Prominent public speakers undergo intense training before they stand before an audience to speak. Those close to figures like presidents and powerful religious leaders will confirm to you that indeed the training can last for several months or sometimes years. The reason this happens is to ensure whatever they speak to the audience is exactly what is in their mind; it could be the truth or just lies. However, one can still read their minds accurately despite vigorous training. The relationship between words and movements can easily sell them out; it is difficult to fake emotions throughout the speech. If someone is narrating a sad event, for example, their movements will be quite different from those associated with an exciting event. Let us analyze the following case.

"Ladies and gentlemen, we are saddened beyond the comprehension of words by the sudden and untimely demise of our brothers and sisters in the ferry that sank on Monday morning. Our gallant men in blue have been working day and night to retrieve the bodies since the tragedy happened. Unfortunately, it breaks my heart to announce to you that all has been an effort in futility. Our intelligence has revealed that the bodies have been buried deep in the murky sea waters, a situation that is complicating the process of retrieving the bodies as we do not have sufficient equipment for such an undertaking. We require more than four tanks of oxygen for each diver; a resource that is not plenty in supply at the moment. We have also come to a logical conclusion that sending those divers to the bottom of the ocean is nothing short of putting their innocent lives at great risk. We have therefore decided to call off the operation to avoid losing more lives. I know this is not the best news for the families of the victims but it is the right thing to do. We shall hold a vigil for the victims by the sea for the next two days. It is not enough but it is the best we can do at this point, our hands are tied."

Let us analyze this speech by a government official about an ill-fated sunken ferry that claimed the lives of all its occupants. We want to try and read the speaker's mind and verify these claims. We shall be in a position to tell whether this is just another ploy to cover up for the government's unwillingness to find the remains of its deceased citizens or there is some logic in it.

"We are saddened"

We know whether this statement is genuine by observing the way the speaker says it and accompanying movements. First of all, the word 'saddened' should be mentioned with a low, dejected and troubled voice. Second, it should be accompanied by a little bow or dilation of the pupils. To emphasize it further, there ought to be a brief silence before the speaker continues.

"Beyond the comprehension of words"

This statement means that words can't explain the feeling, so actions ought to play that role. The speaker could press their lips together or cross their arms to show despair.

"Brothers and sisters"

The look in the face of the speaker as these words come out of mouth should reveal the feeling one would have when talking about the loss of a real brother and sister. Mentioning those words would likely send shivers all over the speaker's body. The lips could tremble, the voice ought to be shaky and they could even choke in their words. If the voice is smooth and clear, then we have reason to doubt the speaker's true feelings about the victims.

"Effort in futility"

This statement implies despair. The speaker's voice should express that, especially when saying the word 'futility'. Body movements

that could be associated with this statement include crossing arms,
slight bowing of the head and bringing feet together.

"Murky"

The literal meaning of this word is dark and gloomy. Regarding
ocean waters, it becomes even scarier. We should pay attention to
the way the speaker says this dreadful word. We expect his face to
show this by looking just like it-dark and gloomy. We need to feel
the pain of saying the word in his voice; is it shaky? We need to
see the pain written on his face. His hands should also speak of the
feeling. Are the fists clutched? Are the fingers crossed? Are the
arms folded around the chest? Look for anything that will show the
dreadful nature of that word.

"Logical conclusion"

The way the speaker says the word 'logical' should tell you
whether the conclusion is indeed a logical one or it is just another
wild claim. The amount of stress applied to the word indicates the
extent of seriousness. If he says it casually, then it means he is just

trying to dupe his listeners with a technical word. Also, does his explanation support the weight of the word? Is it logical that a whole country is unable to acquire enough oxygen for the exercise?

By keenly analyzing some single words used by the speaker, together with his body movements, we will be able to read his mind and ascertain the sincerity of his words. If the speaker had the intention of manipulating this audience, only those equipped with mind-reading skills will escape the snare.

EMOTIONAL MANIPULATION

Emotions are one weakness among human beings that have been used to influence their thinking and behavior for millennia. You have heard of phrases like, 'I didn't plan to do this but love/anger made me do it or, 'I was not going to do that but I was provoked into doing it. This aspect of human nature has been in use in the world of dark psychology to manipulate people into doing things they'd otherwise not do if they acted independently. Strong emotions like love and anger are the most used to achieve this purpose. A manipulator will normally identify an emotion that doubles up as your weakness. They'll then provoke it in you and let everything else flow according to their plan. Manipulators are experts when it comes to presenting their 'facts'. They will overwhelm you well-coated ideas t to support their case. One outstanding characteristic of these ideas is they are highly manipulated to give weight to their argument as well as to entice you to shift your ground. Some of the techniques used by manipulators to put you off balance psychologically include abrupt surprises, unnecessary interruptions, and not giving you enough time to speak. These techniques will likely disorient you to a point that you cannot think straight. This throws your mind in chaos and leaves you exposed and vulnerable. Another technique will involve coming up with complicated procedures that don't serve any purpose. The aim of such procedures is only to confuse you more. Once you cannot figure out where to proceed, the manipulator will pose as the guardian angel that will drag you out of that situation. This gives them another chance to prey on your emotions that are now in shambles to advance their selfish interests. We are going to look at some of these emotions and point out exactly how

manipulates use them to influence your mind.

Love

People are naturally attracted to someone that shows them care and affection. Dark psychologists have perfected the art of feigning this affection to gain the target's trust and attention. The first step will be to let you pour your mind out. This creates a perfect atmosphere to identify your weaknesses. If they don't get all the information from you, they will force it out of you through mind-provoking questions and cues. If you are not very careful, you might end up giving out every bit of information including your highly guarded secrets. The manipulator will try to fill the gaps in your love life as a way of getting you to accommodate them. Once they are in your space, they will be able to monitor and influence your every move. The threat of withdrawing their love becomes a tactic to keep you on track; this technique will likely succeed since they'll have already identified that void of love to be your major weakness. Once they get what they want, a manipulator will start a systematic withdrawal until they cut you off completely.

Anger

This is another emotion that makes people do things they end up regretting. Individuals with a short temper are the easiest target for mind control. All a manipulator needs is a simple provocation and everything else falls into place, just as they expected. Just like in the case of love, a manipulator will identify your weakest point by making you pour out your heart to them. Professionals, more so lawyers, have perfected this technique when it comes to dealing with their opponents in the corridors of justice. They will float mind-provoking questions at you and when you react with unreasonable aggression, they will pick out the most implicating words and statements which they end up using against you. Politicians also have a habit of charging their followers with negative emotions to capitalize on the charged atmosphere to advance their interests. The best way to approach a target to use their anger against them is simply to start an argument. The argument should be centered on the topic that you consider to be very sensitive to them. Try as much as possible to attack their interests in a not very direct manner. Let their anger boil over every word that comes out of your mouth until it explodes. Once their anger takes the better part of them, fan it until they are totally out of control. This 'fanning' should involve creating the illusion that you are trying to calm down the situation while bringing up more provocative ideas in the process. As expected, this uncontrollable anger will impair the victim's ability to think and reason well. This is the best chance to push their thinking to the limit. They will do exactly what you want them to without second thoughts. Another effective way of fanning their anger is by raising your voice and displaying negative emotions such as contempt and sarcasm. This tactic works best when you are the one arguing with them and there is no third party involved. The argument, if you are involved, should not be about winning rather, it should only raise the target's emotion to a point where they are overwhelmed then you can soften your ground to create the illusion of empathy. This will easily make them welcome you in their circles because false empathy is a consolation.

Signs that you are being manipulated emotionally

Emotional manipulation involves relationships and friendships that are one-sided. Unlike true friendships and relationships where love, respect, and accommodation are mutual, manipulative ones are characterized by the dominance of one party where their interests come first. The interests of the target are taken off the table without due consideration. However, the manipulator creates an illusion of fairness and selflessness in front of the target. The following signs should help you to differentiate genuine emotions from manipulative ones.

The battleground has shifted-whenever someone

insists on dragging you to their realm just before a sensitive discussion, be very cautious about their intentions. You will be vulnerable away from your place of comfort such as your home. The power shifts in their favor once they are in their comfort zone, leaving you at a great disadvantage.

Constant criticism of your personality- this is

meant to strip you of your self-esteem and leave you exposed for manipulation. The manipulator tries to find fault in virtually every aspect of your life including personality, opinions, and beliefs. They will attack your convictions but will not give concrete reasons as to why they're doing that. In most cases, they will use a crooked line of reasoning to justify their ideas. This deliberate distortion of facts serves the purpose of keeping you in the dark. Lack of information leaves you with no ability to challenge their ideas or defend your own if challenged.

Turning you against yourself- a manipulator will use your weaknesses against you to get what they want. They do this by creating feelings of guilt within you whenever you make a mistake or are upset about something. If you are quick to anger, for example, a manipulator will provoke your anger and capitalize on it to advance their interest. If you are upset with yourself because you did something you consider being unpleasant, they will make it look very bad thus creating feelings of guilt towards yourself.

NEURO-LINGUISTIC PROGRAMMING

This is a scientific approach to communication that originated in America in the late 20th century. It relates neurology, language and the behavioral pattern of an individual. This aspect of communication is mostly used by dark psychologists to read, influence and manipulate the minds of their subjects. This is a reverse process where the predator first analyses the words of the prey and use them to infiltrate the mind. This way, the predator can program the subject's mind to work exactly as they want it to. All this happens without the knowledge of the victim. There are various modifications of the procedure by the manipulator to tie loose ends to keep the victim in the dark until their mission is

accomplished. This technique should not be viewed entirely in a

bad light as it has been widely used to treat many psychological,

mental, personality, and general health disorders such as phobias,

common colds, depression, and allergies. However, many experts

have classified NPL as pseudoscience due to the inability to prove

its effectiveness in studying the psychology of the human brain.

This does not eliminate this concept as a technique used in the

world of dark psychology to control and manipulate minds. This

chapter will illustrate why this tactic must be on your watch list as

far as psychological manipulation is concerned. This technique

uses various aspects of human thinking and reasoning to function.

First, the manipulator will take note of your physical behavior to

determine which part of the brain you are using more than the rest.

This is achieved through the use of the following:

- Rate of dilation of the pupil

- The rate and pattern of your skin flush

- The most used sense, i.e. smell, sight, and touch

- The behavioral pattern when speaking shows out the

  difference between an individual that is lying and one that

  is telling the truth.

Someone that uses NPL to manipulate you will do everything they can to copy your body movements including posture, sitting position and eye movements. This allows them to determine how your brain responds or reacts to their words. As much as they try to conceal this, you will always notice it if you have a little knowledge of NPL. Try making swift movements and you will notice that they are trying to follow your every move. The best way to deal with someone that is trying to copy your moves is to move your body, especially your eyes, in unpredictable patterns, ones that are hard to copy. You will likely notice their struggles and better still make it impossible for them to use those movements to control your mind.

Allowing someone with the knowledge of NPL to touch you is a huge mistake. They will take advantage of your situation to tap into your emotions. They will wait to see you react to the most emotional aspects of your life. The manipulator will then touch one of your parts deliberately and see how you react to it. This gives them an excuse to get even closer to you and do their thing. If they pretend to be comforting you, for example, the same place they touched you, be it your shoulder or back, will be a reminder of that little feeling when they touch you again. Do not allow someone gets close to you unnecessarily, keeping that distance is important if you sense that someone wants to use NPL to manipulate you.

MIND CONTROL BY CULTS AND MAGICIANS

Sometimes what you think is supernatural is nothing more than a simple trick involving mind control. When confronted by a threatening situation, it is human nature to panic and does things that might be considered irrational. Most cults and black magicians have perfected the act of inducing tension on their victims then use that chaotic situation to take advantage of their weakened mind. With a compromised mind, one can easily make things up, things that the predator intended. When they purport to perform 'miracles', for example, they would first drive you into a panic attack. They will then use obvious things like sweat on your body to create an illusion that it is something else like oil or glittering. Magicians use natural occurrences to take credit as far as their 'magic' is concerned. They use things such as a sudden flash of flight to conceal obvious moves then convince that they have performed magic. They know that the human eye tends to concentrate on bright and conspicuous things so they will use this knowledge to draw your attention from what there are doing. They will act swiftly and before you notice something is happening they will have done it already.

The main tactic used by cults to control the minds of their victims is through deliberate manipulation of facts. They have their way of interpreting even the most obvious of facts. This skewed way of presenting ideas throws the victim into a state of confusion and makes them vulnerable to mind manipulation. A cultist will create the illusion of wanting to help their victim understand something but in the end, it is their interest that gets served. To prevent any objection from their subject, a manipulator will first strip them of their own identity. They will attack their personality both directly and indirectly until the individual loses their identity. This means that they won't be in a position to stand up for what they believe in nor defend their opinions and ideas. The manipulator's line of reasoning becomes the only option to be picked by the victim. Lack of information means the target only consumes what the cultist wants them to.

Cultists and magicians also apply an isolationist policy to their target. When someone is separated from the rest of the population, they become more vulnerable to mind manipulation. The victim(s) are taken to an isolated location where they get indoctrinated and brainwashed without interference from the outside world. You have heard of religious seminars and something of the sort; these are meant to cut the target off from things that would otherwise prevent them from getting manipulated. It also ensures there is sufficient time to brainwash and re-educate them. You should be wary of meetings and workshops that take unusually long in isolated places and run by people you barely know. Chances are such training that has suspicious motives that have something to do with controlling your mind.

This group of mind manipulators normally has a list of strange demands for their victims. Cultists tend to demand spiritual and sometimes bodily purity as a condition to be part of it. These demands go way beyond the ordinary religious practices of established religions. They also put strict measures to conceal their motives such a deliberate refusal to address their subjects' complaints about their dissatisfaction. They also have complicated procedures that are only meant to mislead their victims. Normally, you'd rather skip reading the terms and conditions and click 'agree' anyway. The simple reason is that they are usually lengthy and sometimes hard to understand. This is the case with the way cults and magicians do their things. They will deliberately complicated things because they know such complexity will force you to agree with them and save yourself undue trouble.

HOW TO PROTECT YOURSELF FROM MENTAL MANIPULATION

Everybody can become a victim of mind control and manipulation. I wish to dispel the notion that only weak people can be manipulated by dark psychologists, even the most intelligent people in the society can fall prey. The very first step in protecting your mind from getting controlled is by knowing everything that is there to know about dark psychology and mind control. If you have read through this book, you are in a good position to understand how to effectively shield yourself from mental manipulation. Knowledge of the following will help you come up with appropriate measures to combat mind control:

- The meaning of mind control.
- The techniques used to control people's minds.

- Risk situations that can expose to mind control.

- The kind of people, those that are, capable of controlling your mind.

Having learned the various aspects of mind control, it is now time to equip you with the necessary skills to avoid being a victim of mind manipulation.

Monitor their mood

Naturally, an individual develops a mood that reflects their current situation. In the case of dark psychology, however, the predator will exhibit moods that are quite inconsistent with the situation at hand. They might try to conceal this but they will always give themselves away in one way or another. If you're faced with a sad situation, for example, a manipulator will act as though they are equally saddened but only at the surface. A major characteristic of these moods is that it doesn't last long; it disappears as soon as their objective is met. Someone that usually resents you will act jovial when they want something from you. This is a tactic used to control and manipulate minds.

Don't get isolated

Like we have seen, a manipulator will attempt to isolate their victim to make the process of manipulation easy. Look out for the slightest signs of separation from the rest of the population when meeting or talking about something with someone. Refuse to attend meetings that take place in private spaces such as people's homes or anywhere else that puts you at a disadvantage. Insist on public spaces and places where your access to information or interaction with other people is not limited. Always ensure a couple of your friends know about your whereabouts at any given time. You should also trust these people with the kind of information you consume. Chances are that at least one person will point out to you any suspicious activities happening without your knowledge. Also, when meeting people you barely know, let a friend or relative accompany you to meet them. If the person/people try to isolate you from the person accompanying you, think twice.

Avoid rigid rules and procedures

The world of dark psychology employs uncompromising rules and procedures even where the situation demands. This is meant to turn the target into a zombie that just does what the predator wants because they don't understand how that particular system works. If you notice that a certain entity has strict rules that are hard to change, run away from that place as fast as you can and don't look back.

Pay attention to details

Observe a person's behavior when they talking to you about a sensitive matter. You can look out for verbal and non-verbal cues as you engage them. Are these some words that appear misplaced in their speech? Is their mood consistent with the situation at hand? Does their body speak a different language from their words? This should help you analyze the person very well and know their intentions before you fall for their words. Look out for NPL as you engage someone you suspect might be out to manipulate you. This might be hard to point out but there are a couple of things that might help you spot NPL.

- Is the person trying to copy your posture and body movements?

- Does the person keep asking mind-provoking questions that go beyond a formal setting?

- Does the person give you unsatisfactory answers and explanations?

- Is the person being selfish with information about themselves?

Once you have answered these questions correctly, you should decide whether to proceed with the person or not.

Avoid giving too much information about yourself to the wrong people

It is okay to open up about your problems to someone, but it should not be just anybody. Someone that has the intention of manipulating you will dig in as much information from you as they can. However, they don't do this directly. They will give cues and then allow you to give them the information unknowingly. This gives them a chance to identify your weaknesses and use them to manipulate you. Be very careful with people that ask personal questions yet you barely know them. Some of the problems that make you vulnerable to mind control include:

- Financial difficulties

- Relationship and marital problems

- Health issues

- Being homesick

- Age-related issues as in the case of teenagers and old people

- Being considered a social or societal misfit

The only person that needs to know about these problems, if you have any, is that person you have absolute trust for. Everyone else that tries to dig up such information in you should be treated with suspicion.

Don't succumb to attacks on your identity

Many manipulators will attempt to through you off balance by attacking your personality. This is meant to erode your self-esteem and leave you exposed and vulnerable. Always defend yourself with everything you got because it is your last line of defense against mental manipulation. If you cannot put up a brave fight, you can choose to walk away all together when your pride is still intact. In other words, do not engage individuals that are determined to make you find fault in yourself. Once you conquer attempted attacks on your identity, you will be able to challenge your opponent's ideas as well as defend your own with confidence. The predator will feel challenged and bark off. However, they will always keep coming back until they get what they want, so you need to be always alert.

Beat them in their own game

You can always make a fool out of someone that is trying to fool you. Use reverse psychology to figure out exactly what the would-be-manipulator is up to. Having learned much about dark psychology in the preceding chapters, you are in a better position to notice when someone is trying to manipulate you. Once you have seen their intentions, all you need to do is avoid every trap they set for you. They will feel humiliated and give up trying as soon as they start. Sounds fun, right? Try this with someone fond of playing with people's minds and see how thrilling it is seeing them walk away with their head bowed in shame or better still see how they will be avoiding you like a plague.

DARK PSYCHOLOGY IN DATING

Having learned all the basics about dark psychology, we will now have a look at how individuals use relationships to manipulate others. Research shows that more than 60% of all relationships in the world today are not genuine. They have been initiated by manipulators to take advantage of their target while hiding under the pretense of love. The reasons such relationships are started include; for material gains, religious and social reasons. All these kinds of relationships have one unique characteristic – they always come to an end as soon as the objective is met. You can easily identify these kinds of relationships from the following features.

They are one-sided

From the onset, the victim will be alone in matters that require a collaboration of both partners in the relationship. Whenever the relationship is threatened by outside forces, the predator will not be as restless and worried as their victim. They won't see the kind of damage that will be done by such threats thus will not put up an honest fight to protect it. The amount of input in terms of time and other resources towards the relationship will generally be lower on the side of the predator. Most of the things they do will be because they have been pushed by the 'partner' or other circumstances and not because they are obligated to do them by being a fundamental part of that relationship.

Fluctuating moods

Since it is not from within, the predator might be unable to hide their true feelings once in a while. They might become easily irritated by simple things that otherwise would not be a big issue for people in a relationship. When someone is upset or angry, it becomes difficult to conceal who they are. That is why you will be shocked to hear someone that you have always thought cares about you say strange things to you, things that have been kept secret for months or years. The funny thing about relationships is that things, more so past secrets, have a way of crawling out of their hideouts with a small provocation.

 First of all, the manipulator resents the victim. The resentment will boil over and explode when they cannot hold it any longer.

A complete absence of empathy

Naturally, one is supposed to share in the pain of another, especially the person they love. However, in the case of emotional manipulation, the predator does not have any feelings for the pain of their victim. This is manifested when the victim is undergoing difficulties. The manipulator will be temporarily absent from their lives both emotionally and physically, if anything, they will be glad you're going through such so they can pounce on the opportunity to control you. This tells you that people that use dark psychology to influence others are sociopaths, psychopaths, and narcissists.

However, a manipulator will conceal their motive until that time when their objective is met. They will improvise whenever they are cornered. They might surprise you with a gift, for example, when they see that their lack of affection is about to get noticed. The sooner you discover this kind of relationship means you can bring

it to an end before things get far.

75